FLASH CARDS
便条集

FLASH CARDS
便条集

Yu Jian
于坚

Translated from Chinese by
Wang Ping and Ron Padgett

Zephyr Press & The Chinese University Press
Brookline, Mass. | Hong Kong

Cover image by Xu Bing
Book design by *type*slowly
Printed by Friesens in Canada

Several of these poems have previously appeared in
The Believer, Cipher Journal, and New American Writing.

This publication is supported by the Jintian Literary Foundation. Zephyr Press
also acknowledges with gratitude the financial support of The National
Endowment for the Arts and the Massachusetts Cultural Council.

Published for North America by Zephyr Press, a non-profit arts and education
501(c)(3) organization that publishes literary titles that foster a deeper understanding
of cultures and languages. Zephyr books are distributed to the trade by Consortium Book
Sales and Distribution [www.cbsd.com] and Small Press Distribution [www.spdbooks.org].

Published for the rest of the world by:
The Chinese University Press
The Chinese University of Hong Kong
Sha Tin, N.T., Hong Kong

Cataloging-in-Publication Data is available from the Library of Congress

ZEPHYR PRESS
www.zephyrpress.org

JINTIAN
www.jintian.net

THE CHINESE UNIVERSITY PRESS
www.chineseupress.com

CONTENTS

A NOTE ON TRANSLATING YU JIAN

by Ron Padgett

I first met Yu Jian at a poetry festival in Sweden in the summer of 2002. He was one of five Chinese poets taking part. They read their work in Chinese, followed by translations into Swedish, so my impression of their work was based solely on the sound and manner of the readers. Yu Jian's first reading was in a mysterious, highly charged whisper, which I imagined to be secretly comic. Afterward I approached the Chinese group and asked one of them, who was serving as interpreter, to tell Yu Jian that although I understood no Chinese, I liked his reading very much. He smiled, said thank you, and handed me an anthology of his work in English.

Late that night I browsed through it, until I came to a poem that seemed oddly familiar. The next poem had this same aura, and the third one had lines that I magically anticipated, almost verbatim. My sudden prescience became eery, and then came the credit line: "Translated by Wang Ping and Ron Padgett."

About seven years earlier Wang Ping had asked me to collaborate on some translations for an anthology of contemporary Chinese poetry she was preparing. I was happy to do so, and I found working with her a great pleasure. I liked the poems we translated, but I had forgotten the name of their author—of course, Yu Jian.

The next morning he found this story highly amusing, saying, "Maybe I have translated your poems without knowing it too!" Aha! I quickly foisted a copy of my *New & Selected Poems* on him.

Once he had returned to China and I to the U.S., we began an email correspondence, thanks to the translation program on his computer. Our messages came through in a somewhat cryptic language (in one instance he referred to a borough of New York as "Her Imperial Highnesses' Neighborhood," i.e., Queens). This gave me the idea of writing poems with him via email, using the computer's translation program virtually as a third collaborator. Fifteen poems ensued.

ix

Meanwhile Wang Ping, hearing of my new friendship with Yu Jian, suggested that she and I do more of his poems, so we set out on his modestly titled *Anthology of Notes*. From time to time she emailed me a rough draft from the Chinese and I tarted it up. Sometimes I asked her to clarify words or passages, but her versions usually didn't require a lot of work on my part. On the few occasions that we were perplexed by something in the original poem, we asked Yu Jian for clarification. His answers were invariably along the lines of "Ah, yes, a mystery!" Sometimes I went back and revised our previous versions, always checking with Wang Ping. It was nice to go along without a contract or a deadline, for this way all one has is the pleasure of doing the work.

Throughout, I tried to keep in mind one of the dangers of translating Yu Jian—the temptation to turn him into an American poet. Sometimes he does sound like a combination of William Carlos Williams, Gary Snyder, Frank O'Hara, and me. The opposite temptation is to make him sound "Chinese." My aim was to locate him between these two extremes.

In 2004 Yu Jian visited the U.S. for the first time. He and I went to the top of the Empire State Building alone. I had warned him that all I could say in Chinese is *Hello, chop sticks*, and *thank you*. He had replied that the only things he could say in English are *Hello, chop sticks*, and *thank you*. So before an interpreter joined us later that afternoon, we walked around New York, speaking our respective languages, gesturing, and laughing. During that stay Yu Jian gave a poetry reading at the St. Mark's Poetry Project, for which I read the translations Wang Ping and I had done. It was interesting to see how well his poetry came across to the audience, both in Chinese and in translation.

These personal interactions continued in 2008, when I went to China, for the first time. He and I took part in a poetics conference, sponsored by the Pamirs Academy, which convened a number of Chinese and foreign poets for discussions, poetry readings, and travel together for one week. At the conclusion of the conference, Yu Jian took me to his home town, Kunming, where he and I gave a bilingual reading of our solo and collaborative work, one of the most thrilling readings I've ever been a part of. But it was also an enormous pleasure to meet his family and to pal around with him and his friends as he gave me the grand tour of

Kunming and the surrounding area. Wearing dark Mafioso sunglasses, he cut quite a figure, with his short, chunky build and shaved head, as he briskly strode the streets, dodging traffic, occasionally greeting someone. Apparently he is a rather well-known citizen of Kunming. It was here that I learned that he was the second bestselling contemporary Chinese poet, behind Bei Dao.

But he seems too busy to be caught up in his celebrity. Despite his cell phone, computer, and modern town house, a large part of his attention is focused on China's past, whose memory he yearns to preserve, both the good and the bad. I detect no sentimentality or nostalgia in his desire, only an immense respect for Chinese tradition. Remarkably, he shows no bitterness for the deprivations and humiliations inflicted on him and his family by the Cultural Revolution. Another large part of his attention is devoted to the phenomena immediately before him, whether it be the handlebars of a pink motorscooter or the smell of a warm bun stuffed with sweet bean paste or the wrinkles of the faces of four very old peasant women in rich royal blue costumes. And in much of it he finds a latent humor and a latent sadness that seem the manifestation of the perpetual mystery of life.

After returning from China, I continued to receive more drafts from Wang Ping, as she tried to keep up with Yu Jian's prolific output. His *Anthology of Notes* had burgeoned into a series of books by that title. Finally we realized that we would never catch up with him. It was time to select from our translations and make a book.

What qualifies me to claim to "translate" Yu Jian's work, even with such an able collaborator as Wang Ping? First, at an early age I was strongly influenced by the example of Ezra Pound's translations, he whose Chinese was minimal but whose "River Merchant's Wife: A Letter" has become a classic (despite its liberties with Li Bai's original). In the case of Yu Jian, I believe, perhaps too mystically, that my being a poet allows me to absorb, as if by osmosis, a sufficient amount not only of his work but also of his spirit, though I admit that there is much about him I do not understand. But perhaps in poetry understanding is overrated. I still get more pleasure from "Her Imperial Highnesses' Neighborhood" than from "Queens." Fortunately I have Wang Ping to keep me from going overboard.

FIRM, STEADFAST, STAUNCH, RESOLUTE:
YU JIAN'S FLASH CARDS

by Simon Patton

Poetry, when it works, reminds us our thoughts are seldom our own.

One of the refreshing things about Yu Jian's *Flash Cards* is his awareness of the poetizing of reality in so much so-called poetry. When he first began thinking of himself as a poet, he was still working in a factory in Kunming: his environment at the time was anything but romantic. Yet the poetry that emerged in China as a response to the passing of the Maoist era was, much of it, filled with a yearning for dreams of things that cannot be. His belated first collection *60 Poems*, published in 1989, is dominated by the impulse to bring poetry back to earth: the title itself declares "nothing fancy." Many of the poems were written for friends, and so were topical and idiosyncratic; others tried to confront the realities of everyday living. He has continued to develop this impulse in his work ever since.

In 1993, he wrote an unlikely poem called "The Beer Bottle-top." In it, he tries to confront the unpoeticality of his subject (*with no other entries on it in the dictionary   no original meanings extended meanings transferred meanings*); he finds it stripped of associations that he could exploit for the sake of literature (*but its plight is even more wretched   a cigarette butt reminds the world of a slob / a bone brings to mind a dog or a cat and footprints allude to a human life*), but in this poverty of meaning he is forced to confront the object directly, in all its dangerous particularity: (*all I did was bend down   and pick up this alluring small white object / it was hard   with a serrated rim which cut into my finger   and made me feel a sharpness unlike that of knives.*) Poetry according to this conception offers resistance to prefabricated poem-thoughts and strives to find a non-ordinary language for the ordinary.

In *Flash Cards*, readers are bound to be amused by Yu's merciless attack on the battalions of pseudo-poets who dominate, as they do everywhere, the Chinese literary scene. His main target is metaphor,

metaphor as a deliberate obfuscation of reality for the sake of "poetic interest," for an elusive "meaningful depth": *as to what a pair of deer-skin shoes in a refrigerator means / you'll never be able to guess: footprints in a thawing mountain region / rice symbolizes Asia / while at the appearance of the word "bronze" you're meant to think of / a frivolous old emperor / as for "phoenix-tailed anchovies" what in your world could they possibly correspond to? / "palace maids," of course / spring, need I point out, refers to a green sweater / made from plaited willow twigs and if you can't figure that out / then you are an illiterate totally lacking in imagination.* In a later poem he provides the "secret recipe" for such writing: *The lake takes off its blue mitten / exposing a red palm . . . Next you should compare yourself / to something small and lovely on the shore / a gazelle or deer drinking water.* (p.95) This beautification of the scene mapped out by a dead, conventionalized poetic logic is condemned by Yu because the lake, as a result of modernization, is fast drying up. Finally, in an interesting leap of thought, Yu connects the urge to express one's innermost feelings, the pretext for so much of this metaphorical writing, with a desire to *confess*, a desire that the State is so keen to instill in its subjects.

Another striking feature of both these *Flash Cards* and Yu's work in general is his evocation of *The Waste Land*. His long poem *Flight* is a homage to T. S. Eliot's classic and attempts, in its own way, to write a major poem on the degradation of life in China. It is one of the ironies of Yu's life that one of the most formative events in his personal history — the Cultural Revolution of 1966–1976 — was a time in which both high-brow literary culture and the often-neglected but irreplaceable culture of ordinary street-life suffered annihilation. An obsession with being on the right side of politics, of following the Party line managed to infect a whole society with the insidious mechanism of SUSPICION – SELF-REPRESSION – CONFESSION – SUPPRESSION, a perpetual merry-go-round. Yu writes of this as a basic fact of life: *Don't think we don't know / the secrets hidden deep in / your soul* (p.117). The poems in *Flash Cards* contain memorable images of desolate aggressive progress: the man who leaps from a building in order to experience, if only for a few seconds, the sense of soaring flight systematically denied to him by social "life," the bridegroom in the park who can manage to relax only on his Big Day by composing himself to look like a President who has just added his signature to some important document, a poem about a butterfly in a newspaper stuffed with news about murders and the minute fluctuations of the stock market . . . . *The Waste Land* is a world in which people have dutifully lost their humanity:

> *On the stage*
> *even the flowers are wearing Mao's wooly uniform*
> *The only tenderness is the tea girl*
> *When she walks among the documents and microphones*
> *pouring tea*
> *we realize   that the puppets*
> *have mouths too   (p.127)*

Despite this grim clear-sightedness, Yu remains alive to positive aspects of experience. At the beginning of one stanza, he exhorts poets to stand up as *The golden age is coming soon* (p.129). Yu Jian is always moved by things that have no "productive" use to the world: such things return human beings to their senses and to their emotions. Since the nature in human nature has become so deeply antagonistic towards both itself and the natural world, Yu turns away from the man-made in search of what we have lost. *Over there / the native land / begins / in the local dialect / in the soil / in the naming of a leaf* (p.55). Yu Jian's poetry shivers with an undisguised delight in the wildernesses of his homeland, the province of Yunnan, a place that he has crisscrossed since the 1980s and written about at great length. Unlike the tamed environment of a classical Chinese garden, the landscapes of his home place which attract him most strongly are quintessentially wild. In the role of a loyal subject, he evokes his Queen of Yunnan: *trailing skirts tailored from moonlight / a snake between her lips   an owl / fastened in the bun of her hair   sapphires unearthed by panthers inlaid at her breast* . . . This exuberance, otherness, lushness, energy is in direct contrast to *The Waste Land*. It is no wonder that Yu writes of it with a sense bordering on religious awe.

The crow has been Yu Jian's animal totem throughout his writing life. On the one hand, it shares a close relationship to the darkness of the Wasteland; on the other, it is an exemplification in nature of the vital, marginal dark that brings out the best in humanity. Yu's second collection was named after a major poem called "The Naming of a Crow." In this poem, he works through the metaphors habitually associated with the bird (*this living representative of the powers of darkness, a swan nourished on the everlasting blackness of night, this lawless wild witch-bird*) and celebrates both the inexpressibility of crowhood alongside a powerful sense of affinity. At the same time, it is a symbol of the poetry he would like to write: lacking conventional "beauty" and a musical "song," such poetry would shadow the aestheticizing, anaesthetizing impulses of mediocre lyricism and seek to affirm a place for itself as a raucous, unruly, but real outsider. Like the English poet Edward Thomas' enigmatic "pure thrush word," Yu's crow caw is an intense, individual voice that enlivens reality as it cuts through the cant of wishful thinking:

> *It's possible for ninety poets to think*
> *at the same time*
> *about a crow*
> *about the meaning of its darkness*
> *but when the dark cloud of ninety thousand crows*
> *flies past a crow*
> *it will think of anything*
> *but crows*   (p.61)

It is language that, of necessity, generalizes individuals into types, and that limits the inimitable suchness of any unique being within a reduced repertoire of meanings. This suchness is another facet of Yu's *hei'an* (darkness). This *hei'an* is necessary to the human experience, but not simply a resource amenable to human utility. Another image of the dark summoned in his work is a humble "black pitcher" that is first of all treated as a convenient receptacle for various kinds of metaphorical content: it stands for a young girl's purity, the wizened face of an Egyptian prophet. Yet the pitcher, made, as the poem explicitly tells us, from *a lump of black clay taken from the Earth*, is really only one thing—the employment of emptiness for the containment of water. Here Yu echoes Chapter XI of the Daoist classic the *Daodejing*, one of his favorite books: *Knead clay in order to make a vessel. Adapt the nothing therein to the purpose at hand, and you will have the use of that vessel.* The suggestion is that *hei'an* is the source of that creativeness that sustains and fulfills life, as opposed to the ingenuity that "illuminates" and, in the process, alienates it.

All too often in these poems, the true darkness is the dazzling neon lighting of the contemporary world. He states that the road to death *doesn't lead to a dark coffin or a furnace.* Instead, paradoxically, *It is built with poetic lines / the way / bird's nest dreams / turn into an airport in the light* (p.89)—"airport" epitomizing the homogenous sprawl of the facelessly modern. In the following chilling poem, a "bright" human mass crowds in front of a panther enclosure, pelting the animal with fruit peelings and spitting at it. The poem sides with the cat: *It lies there / above civilization / like a diamond in the dark / disdaining a queen's breast* (p.91).

The intelligent deployment of the powers of feeling is described by Yu as the primary duty of the poet in these "golden years" (years, that is, devoted to the pursuit of gold), lest we, like Midas, become what we admire. As the city around him hardens, he calls on his heart to persist in feeling despite the pain. He is "God's last nerve," left behind in a Concrete City to go on sensing, and to make sense of the turmoil. In this way he lives up to his name: the character *jian* in Yu Jian's name means precisely this: *firm, steadfast, staunch, resolute.* In a recent essay "On Breaking the Lines," he wrote of his desire to transmute despair: "The depth of the darkness determines the degree of brightness. The greatest poets are those with the darkest lives, and so the radiance is dazzling." In *Flash Cards*, we all can enjoy the way Yu brings this blackness to life.

FLASH CARDS

空着手　带着诗
来到他家的客厅　祝贺生日
进门　脱掉鞋子
女士们先生们全部转过身来
像被训练过的猴子　等着
我的手　变戏法似地
掏出一件送给主人的礼物
玫瑰　雪茄　打火机
布娃娃或者牛奶糖
就是开来一辆轿车
他们也会准备好　哇
地一声　"好漂亮哦！"
我忽然明白　在这儿
我的礼物已经拿不出手
我无法告诉这位喜气洋洋的主人
生日　我带来了诗歌
它是那么不合时宜　古老　破旧　陌生
可笑　寒酸　那么匪夷所思
众目睽睽　我的诗歌
就要象一只讨厌的蟑螂那样
引起一阵可怕的
尖叫

I arrive at his living room   with a poem
to celebrate his birthday
I take off my shoes at the door
All the ladies and gentlemen turn to me
like trained monkeys   waiting
to see   what present
I'll pull out like a magician
rose   cigar   lighter
doll   milk chocolate
or a car
They're all ready to say   Wow
How beautiful
Suddenly I realize
I can't show them my present
can't tell the glowing host
that for his birthday   I brought a poem
It's so untrendy   old   shabby   strange
so silly   cheap   unthinkable
Under everyone's gaze   my poem
like a roach
is going to make them
scream in terror

开头是一只兔子
就知道后面有大灰狼
总以为这个剧院必有出口
时间还早　还可以再看下去
再等等　也许会出乎预料
有一辆坦克会横穿过舞台
直到大灰狼来了　才决心离开
可是开头已经不见了　没有兔子
我只能从大灰狼这里出去

In the beginning is the rabbit
Then you know the wolf will follow
We assume a theater must have an exit
It's still early   keep watching
Wait a bit longer   you might be surprised
A tank might drive across the stage
I will stay   till the big gray wolf comes
But now the beginning is gone   so is the rabbit
The only exit is through the wolf

我看见一朵玫瑰
就是说
我看见一朵玫瑰
在它的枝上
我看见一朵玫瑰
就是说
那不是一个姑娘
在她的闺房里
这是完全不同的
两种看法
当你的看见一朵玫瑰
你看见的就是一朵玫瑰
当你看见一位姑娘
你看见的是
两只圆滚滚的乳房
或者同样令人激动的脖子
只有中文系毕业的眼睛
才会对乳房视而不见
才会对少女的脖子视而不见
才会把夏日大街上的姑娘啊
看成一朵有刺玫瑰

I see a rose
That is
I see a rose
on a stem
I see a rose
That is
it's not a girl
in her room
These are two
totally different concepts
When you see a rose
what you see is a rose
nothing else
When you see a girl
what you see
are two round breasts
or her neck that is equally exciting
Only the eyes that graduated from a Department of Chinese
will not see her breasts
or her neck
Only they will mistake the girl on the street in summer
for a rose with thorns

干活的时候
总是有什么在后面或旁边
默不作声地看着
或许还做做鬼脸
但没有时间去对付它
它可能是某种尚未长出舌头的东西
它将在我干完之后
长出舌头

When I work
something always lurks behind me or to the side
watching in silence
making an occasional face
when I'm too busy to chase it away
This thing
is waiting to grow a tongue
after I'm done

棕榈树住的土地被卖掉了
住在它周围的人都在搬家
每一家都用卡车来运载家具
但棕榈树没有地方可搬
它等着被砍倒　烧掉

The property where the palm tree lives has been sold
The neighbors are moving away
Their furniture fills up truck after truck
The palm tree has no place to go
It's waiting to be chopped down   and burned

剃光头的人　和大家一起坐在会议室里
所有的人都看清楚了他的脑袋
但他们都留着头发　梳成各式各样
看不见他们的头　只知道
是王主任的发型
是李科长的发型
是小李的发型
是曼莉的发型
剃光头的人是勇敢的
因为他一根头发也没有
还要和头发一起开会

With a shaved head   he sits in the meeting
Everyone can see his scalp
Everyone else has hair   in different styles
You can't see what's inside   the only thing visible is
Director Wang's hair
Sector Chief Li's hair
Little Li's hair
Manli's hair
The bald one is a brave man
Hairless
He attends the meeting with the haired

一棵树
与天空保持着距离
与另一棵树保持着距离
与另一类果实保持着距离
与另一片土壤保持着距离
与另一片水源保持着距离
与另一群鸟保持着距离
它必须与一切事物保持距离
它只要移动一步　它就丧失天空
丧失土壤　丧失水　丧失鸟
它就丧失职位
它只有死掉

A tree
keeps its distance from the sky
keeps its distance from another tree
keeps its distance from another kind of fruit
keeps its distance from the earth
from water
from birds
It must keep its distance from everything
One single move   it will lose the sky
the soil   water   birds
It will lose its place
It will die

早上　刷牙的时候
牙床发现　自来水已不再冰凉
水温恰到好处
可以直接用它漱口
心情愉快　一句老话脱口而出
"春天来了"

Morning   time to brush my teeth
My gums discover   the tap water is no longer
ice cold
temperature just right
great for rinsing
Joyfully   an old sentence jumps out
"Spring is here!"

把春天比喻成神庙
又一首诗可以开张

绿色的新袍　把神
一个个　打扮成树的样子
诸神登堂入室　高踞山冈
将要繁花似锦　更坚守朴素
万籁俱寂　花朵在树叶中升起
一张张圣洁的嘴唇打开了
朝向一切耳朵
但它们什么也没有说
只是把无言的嘴唇张开

把春天说成神庙　把树说成神祇
只是一个非法的比喻
我只有比喻而已
也许会有人因此改变想法
收起斧子　开始倾听

If I compare spring to a temple
a new poem begins

Green robes   dress gods
as trees
They enter   settle on mountain tops
become flowers   keep simple forms
in silence   flowers rise from leaves
sacred mouths open
towards ears
but nothing comes out
only opened mouths   wordless

To compare spring to a temple   to say a tree is a god
both are illegitimate metaphors
but metaphor is all I have
Someone might change his mind
put down his ax   and start listening

一封信
从用英语写作的某地
一大群维多利亚时代的羽毛中脱离出来
以鸟类姿势　进入邮政局
漂过秋天中的罗马
绕过冰雪的俄国和波兰
横越阳光灿烂的埃及　从印度往东
在汉语管辖的黄昏
抵达另一个邮政局

邮递员　从天空中落下来
把这根白色的羽毛递给我
一封信　千里迢迢
不是向我解释《尤利西斯》
只为了告诉我
我的字　有一个人
看懂了

A letter
slipped away from a pile of Victorian feathers
from a place where English is spoken and written
It entered the post office
in the manner of a bird
flew over Rome in autumn
past icy Russia and Poland
across sunny Egypt   then to the east of India
and arrived at the office at dusk
governed by Chinese

The postman   descended from the sky
handed me the white feather
A letter   traveled a thousand miles
not to explain *Ulysses*
but to let me know
that somebody understood
my words

通向那里的道路不需要经过
铁
塑料和尼龙
不需要经过
街道
和公路
不需要经过
女人的梳妆台
和男人们的啤酒杯
通向那里的道路
不需要证件
鞋子
和汽油
我知道这条道路曾经
在大地上
无边无际地存在
但我现在要去那里
如果我不想踩着
煤气管或者会计室
我只能用诗歌
做我的脚

The road that goes there does not need to go past
iron
plastic and nylon
streets
highways
need nor pass
women's dressing tables
men's beer glasses
The road that goes there
doesn't require ID cards
shoes
gas
I know this road once existed on earth
borderless
but if I want to get there today
and if I don't want to step on
gas pipes or accounting offices
I'll have to travel by poetry
on foot

你将要　完成
成为一朵白玫瑰
即使你曾经在黑暗中
体验着绝望　学会了嚎叫
即使你把所有通向四月的
管道　茎脉
都用墨水和大麻　阻塞
即使你曾经恶毒地
诅咒过　空气　阳光和水
即使你的全部精神
都与玫瑰的图纸
背道而驰
即使你曾经在
天亮之前
演习了自杀

你注定要完成
你注定要成为一朵玫瑰
哦　光明是不可抗拒的
它将在四月准确而规则地进入
你早已残缺不全的黑暗
哦　白玫瑰
你会象一朵
玫瑰
那样开放
完成
按时向蜜蜂纳税
按时向诗人贡献隐喻
按时凋谢

You're about   to become
to be
a white rose
even though you felt despair
in darkness   learned how to scream
even though you blocked
all the paths to April
with ink and weeds
even though you cursed
air   sun   water
even though your spirit
completely goes against
the map of the rose
and you once practiced suicide
at dawn
you are destined to become
a white rose
Oh   the irresistible light
will enter April on time
and you will turn into broken darkness
Oh   white rose
you'll bloom
like a rose
complete
pay a tax to bees on time
provide metaphors to poets on time
wither on time

我在秋天写作　象古代的大师
在八月十五或九月十五
在立秋之日或白露时分
我在秋天写作
这仅仅是一个文雅的好习惯
周围并没有任何迹象
与唐诗中记录的秋天有关
也有一个统治着一切的庞然大物
在天空和大地之间　辽阔地盘踞
但那不是秋天
不是田野上的仙鹤　不是风暴中的牧笛
哦　那在八月无所不在的
是自来水厂的管道　是生锈的
水表　在公寓的一角
计算着　潮湿的面积

I write in autumn   like the ancient masters
on the lunar day of August 15 or September 15
beginning of autumn or White Dew
I write in autumn
A refined habit
nothing to do with
the autumn in Tang dynasty poems
There's something huge that rules everything
between the sky and the earth   its territory vast
but it's not autumn
not cranes over the fields   not a shepherd boy's flute in a storm
What permeates this month
are the pipes from the water treatment plant   and rusty
water meters   on apartment walls
their dials turning

洗衣机的星期六
旋转的快感　将主人的布磨损
磨损它的鲜艳　磨损它的粗糙
磨损它不适应于宴会的部分
磨损　让人日复一日　保持干净
幸福的是一件羊毛衣
它要求与众不同的转速
它的愿望　是与女主人的
红裙子　匹配

The washing machine on Saturday
the pleasure of spinning   wear and tear of the master's clothes
their colors   and roughness
wears out the pieces that aren't right for a banquet
wear and tear   to keep things clean   day in and day out
Happiness belongs only to a cashmere sweater
that demands a different spin cycle
its only wish   to match
the mistress' red skirt

女诗人主持会议
她不知道如何开场
她的诗歌在远方
种植在黑豹子农场
时间到了　开会的人都在看手
女诗人说　全体起立
奏国歌

The poet is hosting a meeting
but she doesn't know how to begin
Her poems are far away
planted at Black Leopard Farm
Time's up   everyone is looking at the clock
"Stand up, everyone"   she says
"Let's sing the national anthem"

用它盛鲤鱼　盛公爆鸡丁
蓝色的龙纹模仿着商代
式样古典的瓷盘
来自往昔的日常生活
使当代的晚餐　获得升华

盛鸡汤的时候　有人手指一滑
它砰地一声　摔裂成了两半
算啦　这盘子不贵　主人叫道
日常生活的悲剧
在史诗中开始　于平庸中结束

It's used for holding carp   gongbao chicken
imitation blue dragons from the Shang Dynasty
The antique bowl
from ancient daily life
glorifies   the dinners of our time

When it got used for chicken soup   someone slipped
it fell   broke in two
Never mind   cried the host   it's a cheap plate
Daily life
began with an epic   ended in tragedy

在怒江州的丛林中一只鹧鸪在尖叫
它的叫声不会惊动躺在树下睡眠的孟加拉虎
也不会惊动傈僳人的树神

但它的叫声会惊动一位诗人的耳朵
惊动　他戴着助听器的耳朵

In the Nu River forest a partridge calls
Its cry won't wake up the tigers of Bangladesh
or disturb the tree gods of the Lisu
but it will startle the hearing aid
in the poet's ear

The Lisu: an ethnic minority in China

在白色的公寓附近
唯一的一棵桉树
令我的记忆完全模糊
我记不得它是在我开始之前就生在这里
还是为了拍卡通片
暂时将它移植

The lone white eucalyptus tree
near the white apartment building
my memory totally at a loss
I can't remember if it was there before I was born
or if I've moved it there temporarily
for a film cartoon

这首诗曾经存在
写的是一个活着的人
但我现在对此人的看法改变了
我删除了这首诗全部痕迹
就象暴君
枪决了失宠的大臣

Originally this poem was written
for a living person
but my view of this person has changed
I have erased every single trace of the poem
like a tyrant
who executes a minister he no longer favors

在超级市场卖音响器材的营业员
不知道什么是抗阻
也不能回答顾客的问题：
丹麦和德国的音箱
哪一个更适合于欣赏蓝调？
不务正业的营业员
他只知道正在喇叭里播送的南方民谣
是来自他遥远的故乡
那高高的高黎贡山中
他父亲和母亲悬挂在山坡上的苞谷地

The salesman who sells sound equipment in the supermarket
has no idea what a fuse is,
cannot answer a customer's question:
The Danish or German hi-fi system —
which is better for the blues?
The unprofessional salesman
can tell you only that the southern folksong on the loudspeaker
comes from his hometown far away,
from the Gong Mountain in Gaoli
where his parents' cornfields hang on high slopes

啊　秋天来了
我不是告诉你
我有一颗悲哀的心
我不是告诉你
我在想念　高高的苍穹
树叶和乌云又起飞了
我只是告诉你
这曾经是　一首古老史诗的开头
后面跟着南方的森林　火焰
跟着鹰　巫师　和弓箭
跟着那些将要成为诗人的人

Autumn is coming
I'm not trying to say
I have a heavy heart
I'm not trying to say
I miss   the high sky
the flying leaves and clouds
I just want to tell you
this was once   the beginning of an old epic
followed by forests in the South   fire
followed by eagles   wizards   bows and arrows
followed by those who would become poets

在我的窗子外面
是另一栋房子的窗子
在我的阳台外面
是另一套房间的阳台
在我的三套间外面
是另一个三套间
在我的单位外面
是另一个单位
在我外面
是另一个象我一样活着的人
我看的风景他也看
我听的声音他也听
我睡觉的时间他也睡觉
我出门的时候他也出门
我们因为同一份文件
在各自的单位上传达
分配到同样规格的房子
有了同样的长方形阳台
我们站在窗子前
互不相识　会心微笑

Outside my window
is the window of another building
Outside my balcony
is the balcony of another apartment
Outside my three-bedroom unit
is another three-bedroom unit
Outside my company
is another company
Outside myself
is another person living just like me
He sees what I see
hears what I hear
When I go to bed, he's going to bed too
When I leave home, he's also going out
We pass the same official document around
in our respective work units
We're assigned to the same style of housing
with exactly the same rectangular balconies
We stand at our windows
strangers, but smile knowingly at each other

无产者在星期日的大街上走
他的眼睛不是坚定地看着前方
而是犹豫不决地经常垂向地面
他想发现一个他决不会弯腰捡起来的
皮夹子

A member of the proletariat walks down the street on Sunday
He does not look straight ahead resolutely
From time to time he lowers his eyes to the ground
He wants to find a wallet
that he will absolutely not pick up

(写到 54　发现缺 37
把 15 割为两首
收获的方法之一)
秋天　一个报废的单词
没有篮子和干草车的单词
没有土地和种籽的单词
没有鸡和狗的单词
没有劳动和收获的单词
秋天　这是一个盲人想象中的电视机
明眼人疯狂时捏造的卧室

Finishing poem #54   I discovered there is no 37
So I cut 15 in half
(a harvesting method)
Autumn   a discarded vocabulary
a word that has lost   baskets and hay carts
land and seeds
chickens and dogs
a word that is void of work and harvest
Autumn   has become a television in a blind man's imagination
a bedroom designed by a madman

闹钟不报告另一类的时间
不报告上帝的死期
不报告农民起义的日程
不报告母狼怀孕的时刻
小闹钟　在我的桌子上　一圈一圈
切削着我的时间　象切削
一只装在车床上的铸铁
它最终要把我车成一只
合格的螺丝
它不告诉我
我最终被一只扳手拧紧
会在什么年龄

The alarm clock doesn't ring another kind of time
Its alarm doesn't announce the death of God
or set the schedule of peasant uprisings
or a wolf's pregnancy
The hands   of the little alarm clock
on my desk   go round and round
slicing my time   as if slicing
into a small block of iron clamped onto it
Its goal is to cut me
into a fine screw
but it won't say
at what age
a screwdriver will draw me down tight

有人发现了西双版纳
"一个美丽的地方"
当地的居民不知道这是什么话
在他们的故乡　他们从未发现什么美丽
世界啊　本来就是这个样子
本来就叫做　西双版纳

Someone discovered Xi Shuang Ban Na
"Beautiful Place"
The locals don't know what that means
They've never discovered beauty in their native land
The world   has always been like this
The place has always been called   Xi Shuang Ban Na

国家公路　依据某些经验和原则
结束于峡谷的险峻
终止于河流的急湍
穷途末路
也是普通话的边境

世界到此为止　再往那边
故乡
在土著人的口语中
沿着天空下的大地
从一片树叶的命名
开始

According to both theory and practice
a national highway
always ends at a steep canyon
always stops at a swirling river
a dead end
the border line for Mandarin
The world ends here

Over there
the native land
begins
in the local dialect
in the soil
in the naming of a leaf

秋天深了
这是诗歌中的废话之一
秋天深了
这是劳动的深度之一
那些种植在深处的东西
现在已经赤裸裸地
呈现于　大地的表面

将有更多的活计要干
大地上的土著们
不会为粮食的成熟伤心
拿着镰刀和绳子
暴露出肌肉中原始的力量

他们要把在前些日子
诗人们大肆歌咏的
所谓青春的　牧歌中的
被用来象征　人性的东西
彻底地伤害

Autumn is deep
In poetry it's a cliché
Autumn is deep
For working people this means how far down
the seeds have been planted
and are now coming up through the surface
naked

More work to be done
The farmers
do not get melancholy about the harvest
They pick up sickles and ropes
their muscles flexing primal power

They mow down
the so-called feelings and youthfulness
that poets have sung like mad
in their pastoral odes

要把每一句话都说得深刻
并且富于哲理
很简单　只要你每一次都把眼睛
用亚麻布蒙起来
然后　想象你是在举着灯
往高处走　象一条鲨鱼那样思考

If you want to make every word you say full of meaning
full of philosophy
it's not that hard   you need only
blindfold yourself
and imagine that you are walking uphill
with a flashlight   and thinking like a shark

九十个诗人会在同一时刻
在黑暗的意义上
想起同一只乌鸦
但九万只乌鸦组成一片移动的黑暗
飞越过一只乌鸦
也不能令这只乌鸦想起
"乌鸦"

It's possible for ninety poets to think
at the same time
about a crow
about the meaning of its darkness
but when the dark cloud of ninety thousand crows
flies past a crow
it will think of anything
but crows

超级市场的水泥地基打入地层十米以下
为的是不使消过毒的苹果和冰冻的牛肉
从货架上掉下来

超级市场　仍旧是大地上的一部分
在这坚固而没有细菌的地面上
长不出苹果树
在这丰富多彩的货架中间
不会有人
在转过某个弯的时候　悠然瞥见
远远的南山下　一头母牛和一头小牛
在低头吃草

The supermarket's concrete foundation goes down ten yards deep
so the sterilized apples and beef
won't fall off the shelves

Supermarket   still part of the earth
No apple trees will grow
out of this solid germless ground
Among the colorful shelves
no one
will see   as he turns the corner
a cow and its calf grazing
on the distant southern mountain

这就是旋转木马
哦　它也出现在中国的公园里了
交给卖票的　两块钱
把小女儿抱上去
木马啊　开始旋转
世界变形　失去了形象
变成她的水彩盒
爸爸　你成了一根线
小骑手高兴得直喊

我不能上去旋转
我害怕那木马停下来的时候
我就成为白痴

Oh   this is the merry-go-round
Finally it has come to the parks of China
Hand two yuan   to the attendant
Lift my little girl up
The wooden horse   starts going around
The world blurs   its original image gone
turned into a box of crayons
Daddy   you're as skinny as a thread
my little rider shouts happily

I can't get on one of those horses
I'm afraid I'd look like an idiot
when it stops

黑暗将至的动物园
蝙蝠在尖叫
我遇见老妇人
站在一排铁栏杆前
望着已经漆黑一团的狼笼
她转过头来的时候
我发现　她有一张
涂着脂粉的　狼脸
她用普通话对我说
下班了　同志

In the zoo where dark is falling
and bats are squeaking
I see an old woman
in front of an iron fence
gazing into the dark wolf cage
When she turns
I see a wolf face
with heavy make-up
In perfect Mandarin   she says
Good evening, comrade

怒江州的黑夜是陌生的
我不知道进入这片黑暗的地图
我的智慧和眼睛一样黑暗
我只有早早地
象盲人一样　睡觉

但对于一头
正在这黑夜中运动的　豹子
智慧象黑暗一样
并不存在

Night along the Nu River is strange
I don't have a map that reaches the darkness
My wisdom is as dark as my eyes
All I can do is go to bed
early   like a blind man

But for a leopard
that prowls at night
there is no need
for wisdom
to exist

在旋转木马的核心
装配着圆形的镜子　目的明确
为的是让骑马的国王能看见自己
镜子比现实宽容
当国王旋转　显影在镜子中
木马也一样旋转
在镜子中　显影
他要看见自己
就要看见木马
他下来　就什么也看不见
国王的旨意　全国惟命是从
但是被一匹木头的马
完全歪曲

In the middle of the horse going round and round
is a round mirror   Its simple goal
is to allow the emperor to see himself as he rides
The mirror is more tolerant than reality
When the emperor goes around   his shadow is in the mirror
So is the wooden horse   going around
If he wants to see himself
he has to see the horse also
When he gets off   he will see nothing
The emperor's orders   are obeyed by the entire country
but completely distorted
by a wooden horse

诗人走在叙事诗的路上
在他身边的　是他的
女读者　她挺着
被白裙子遮住的
大肚子
诗人啊　你要当父亲了

诗人说　这种事情不重要
重要的问题是
捕捞蝌蚪
是在变态的妇产科
还是在抒情的氧气室

The poet walks on the road of narrative poetry
Next to him   is an admirer
her belly swollen
under her white skirt
Poet   you're going to be a father

A trivial matter   says the poet
I'm more concerned with where we should catch the tadpole:
in the grotesque gynecology department
or the lyrical oxygen room

疯人院的设计师
也就是　设计
千家万户　以及
公共厕所和超级商场的
那一位
头脑正常的好人
他用了同样的
砖混结构　玻璃和钢材
同样装修　同样绿化　同样
通煤气和自来水
疯人院　就是一幢正常人设计的
正常建筑

他应该好好地安顿下来
按照作息时间表　坐享现成
当一个正常睡眠
正常进餐的好人

但他不正常　他住在里面
却有一种不正常的想法
他把好人视为正常的房间
当成发疯的 2004 号

发疯的喷塑墙和发疯的钢栅栏
发疯的茶色玻璃窗子和自来水
发疯的无线电收音机和牛皮腰带
发疯的 60 瓦电灯泡

The architect for the madhouse
also designed
thousands of homes
public bathrooms and supermarkets
That kind and normal man
used the same bricks   glass and steel
the same interiors   same lawns and gardens
same gas and running water
The madhouse is normal architecture
by a normal architect

He should settle down
go to bed on time   enjoy what he has
be a good person
who sleeps and eats like a regular guy

But he's not regular   in this regular building
he has irregular thoughts
He regards the normal room
as mad room 2004
mad plastic walls and mad steel fence
mad tinted windows and running water
mad radio and leather belt
mad 60-watt light bulbs
mad folding chairs and porcelain toilet
mad living room with safety gate
mad father   reading a pile of mad papers
mad mop peeling the skin off the concrete floor

发疯的钢折椅和陶瓷小便槽
发疯的大客厅和防盗门
发疯的父亲　在翻一大堆发疯的报纸
发疯的拖把　在剥水泥肉的皮

所以他是疯子
必须把他关在这个
正常的房间里

That's why he's a lunatic
who must be kept
in this normal room

有些东西被搁在黑暗的最高一层
和圣经的精装本放在一起
在一米七五的身高中
我象野心勃勃的马匹那样
服用各种毒草
等待着
再长出毒瘤般的一节

Certain things are placed on the darkest and highest shelf
together with the leather-bound Bible
and I   eager as a horse
with my 5 foot 10 inch height
eat all sorts of poisonous grasses
expecting
a tumor to grow

有一种快感我从未体验
有一种快感希特勒从未体验
他只能命令将军们去干这样的事
我只能在写作中一意孤行
但我们都不能体验
那是洗衣机的快感
不锈钢的缸体　把一切纺织物都视为
肮脏
把少女的内裤视为　污点
把婴儿的手帕视为　细菌
把劳动者的工作服视为
藏垢纳污之所
把旗袍和燕尾服视为
要洗一洗的
它的看法获得全人类
无一例外的支持
于是
为了一个清洁卫生的世界
它把花花绿绿　形形色色的纺织品
东方的丝绸和西方的亚麻布
全部　纳入
黑色的缸体
洗衣机　日日夜夜
在世界的每一个家庭中　旋转
河流会枯竭　政权会垮台
但永远不会有
斯大林格勒战役发生
让一部不能区别头巾和军装的
洗衣机
停下来

There's a pleasure I've never experienced
a pleasure not experienced even by Hitler
who knew only how to order his generals around
like me, who knows only how to cling to writing
neither of us knows
the sensation of a washing machine
its immaculate body   regarding everything
as dirt
A girl's underwear is seen as stain
a baby's handkerchief   germs
a worker's uniform
as a place where grime hides
dresses and tuxedos as things
that must be drycleaned
The whole world supports
its opinion
therefore
to create a clean world
fabrics of all colors and styles
Asian silk and western linen
are thrown into
this dark cylinder
Day and night   the washing machine
spins   in every household on earth
Rivers dry up   thrones fall
but nothing
not even the Battle of Stalingrad
could make it stop
the washing machine
that knows no difference between a hat and an army uniform

明月降临
诗人等待着灵感

就象飞机场的护士
打开了白被单
等待着患急诊的乘客

就象木乃依
在塔克拉玛干的沙漠里
等待着考古队员的
指甲

Under the moon
the poet waits for inspiration

like a nurse at the airport
white sheet folded back
waiting for a patient

like mummies
in the desert
waiting for the fingernails
of archaeologists

红色光芒
飞越车间
工人们　表情庄严
象是一群使徒
在等待着上帝
出炉

Red lights
fly across the factory
and the workers look serious
like disciples
waiting for God
to come out of the furnace

又是秋天　诗歌召唤过的事物
一一造访
西风　帘子
比菊花更瘦的诗人
在九月底凑齐
就象小学班同学
十年后的集会
第五十三名　李清照同学
也上了车

但小学没有在同学中出现
就象诗歌没有再次在事物中出现
三十五岁的李清照
拿出一包话梅　请大家吃

Another autumn   things called forth by poetry
are visiting again
west wind   curtain
poet thinner than chrysanthemums
They gather at the end of September
like an elementary school reunion .
Classmate Li Qingzhao   No. 53
also got on the bus

but the elementary school didn't arrive
just as poetry didn't reappear there
Li Qingzhao   35 years old
treats everybody   to pickled plums

死亡的道路
并不通向黑暗中的棺材或者焚尸炉
而是由优美的诗句筑成
例如

那些鸟巢的梦
是在光辉中变成飞机场

The road to death
doesn't lead to a dark coffin or a furnace
It is built with poetic lines
the way
bird's nest dreams
turn into an airport in the light

黑豹子
犹如黑色石头
在黑暗之中
蕴藉着两颗绿钻石

灿烂的人群在铁栅外面
围住它
向它投掷果皮　向它啐

它一动不动
对人类的文明不屑一顾
犹如黑暗中的钻石
拒绝着女王的胸脯

A black leopard
like a black rock
brewing two green diamonds
in the darkness
a bright crowd outside the iron fence
surrounding it
throwing peels   spitting
It lies there
above civilization
like a diamond in the dark
disdaining a queen's breast

古代的肺在工业的天空尖叫
它被人民日异月新的假牙
一立方一立方地咬穿
在剩余的肺叶内部
杜甫在金属的手术台上
等候一次性切除

诗歌在抒情的厨房里烹制
才子们娴熟地应用形容词
就象应用味精
然后象流行的抽油烟机那样
深度呼吸

Ancient lungs screech in the industrial sky
Fake human teeth
punch holes inch by inch
inside the remaining lungs
Tu Fu lies on the operation table
waiting for a sex change

Poetry is cooking in the romantic kitchen
where talented men sprinkle adjectives
like MSG
then inhale
like a brand-name exhaust fan

(诗歌秘方)

湖泊脱去了蓝色的手套
露出红色的巴掌

蓝色的手套比喻的是湖水
红色的巴掌比喻的是湖盆
接下来　你要把自己比喻成
岸上的某种"可爱的小东西"
斑羚或者水鹿　正在饮水
你可不能把自己比喻成鱼类
它们完蛋了　这个湖正在干涸

94

(Poetry Recipe)

The lake takes off its blue mitten
exposing a red palm

The blue mitten is a metaphor for the lake
The red palm is the lakebed
Next   you should compare yourself
to something small and lovely on the shore
a gazelle or deer drinking water
but don't ever compare yourself to a fish
because they're doomed   the lake drying up

狼经过山谷
辨别植物和食物的声音
哲学家经过同一山谷
作为有思想的食物区别于一切食物
但狼看不见任何思想
它直取食物

A wolf passes through the valley
listening to the sounds between plants and food
A philosopher passes through the same valley
thinking food above the other edibles
but the wolf does not see thoughts
and heads for the food

寒流袭击城市
三点钟　天空已灰暗
冷气控制着一切
有人对生活产生畏惧
有人对旅行丧失了信心
有人把外衣裹紧
但是只要有美丽的女人在附近出现
只是她们的背影在公共场合出现
控制一切的就会立即失控
生活的就想重新生活
旅行的就想继续旅行
那个怕冷的昆明男子
忽然间松开了衣领
露出被严寒冻红的脖子

A cold front is attacking the city
3 p.m. the sky is turning gray
Cold has gripped everything
Someone starts to be afraid of life
Someone loses interest in travelling
Someone pulls his coat tighter
but when a beautiful woman appears
even if it's just a glimpse of her back in the street
the controlling force loses its grip
life wants to live again
the traveler feels like taking off now
and the Kunming man who hates cold weather
suddenly lets go of his collar
revealing his neck, pink from the cold

迪麻洛河
在这儿没有道路一词
从此到彼
只是开始与结束
一只豹在世界跃过
森林合拢

Along the River Dimaluo
there's no such a word as path
From here to there
there's only beginning to end
A leopard leaps across the world
and the forest closes shut

阳光在下午
穿过家具　进入房间的深处
照亮了橱柜里的碗和盘子
照亮了煤气炉上的盐巴瓶和胡椒
照亮了桌面底下的方榫头
阳光重新布置了什物间的光谱
在黑色的一闪中
我忽然发现了那把失踪已久的
银调羹

The afternoon sun
sweeps across the furniture   deep into the room
lights up the bowls and plates in the cupboard
the salt and pepper shakers on the gas stove
and the square stool under the table
The sun rearranges the colors in the pantry
A flash in the darkness
I find the long-lost
silver spoon

十八岁的大学女生
在春天的清早去教室
她的腮帮红红的　她的
长腿裹在毛呢裙子里
只露出野生的一小截
漂亮的女生　高耸着胸脯
双手捧着一瓶茶水
书夹在手肘底下
她目不斜视地穿过
花枝招摇的花园
她要赶去教室
学习哲学

An eighteen-year-old college girl
walks to class on a spring morning
rosy cheeks   long legs
inside a wool skirt
only a small wild part revealed
beautiful girl   chest held high
a cup of tea between her hands
a book beneath her elbow
crossing the flower garden
looking straight ahead
she is rushing to catch
a philosophy class

蝴蝶在花园的睫毛上
捕捉着傍晚的光线
今天的晚报送来了
在凶杀案件和股票行情之间
刊登了一首歌颂这昆虫的诗

On the garden's eyelashes
a butterfly is catching the twilight
The evening paper has arrived
Among reports of murder and the stock market
is a poem about the butterfly

汽车在高原上飞驰
原始森林的边缘出现的时候
一头虚构的野鹿
窜进我的内心
但我没有草地和溪流
让它长久地逗留

The car zooms across the high plateau
When the edge of the virgin forest appears
an imaginary doe
leaps into my heart
but I no longer have a stream or meadow
to keep it there

公元 1998 年
青蛙之国灭亡
故乡的浅草池塘
死亡
只有蚊子继续穿越夏天
间或
也用英语交谈

In 1998
the frogs died
So did the shallow weedy pond
Now all summer long
only the mosquitoes keep flying
sometimes conversing in English

玉花对他说
你太粗糙了
那天在翠湖公园
当着大家的面
你居然摸我的手
真坏
然后在他的头上打了一下

You're too vulgar
says Jade Blossom
that day in Jade Lake Park
You touched my hand
in front of everybody
Bad boy
Then she taps him on the head

我总是想抵达皮带的第七个扣
在第七扣　我的腰围
才符合公有制的标准
但在第九扣我最舒适　最放松
象河马　象漫过河马的洪水
但一生我都在为第七扣斗争
象阴谋　象肚皮后面
永不溃败的阴谋

I always try to reach the seventh hole in my belt
Only at the seventh hole   would my waist
reach the communist standard
But I feel more comfortable at the ninth hole   more relaxed
like a rhino   and the river that flows over him
But I keep struggling toward the seventh hole
like a conspiracy   undefeatable
behind my own belly

你要老实交代
把问题说清楚
不要以为我们不掌握
暗藏在你灵魂深处的
秘密　就是这种交代
供出了国家的敌人
也就是这种交代
造就了抒情诗

You must confess honestly
Reveal all your problems
Don't think we don't know
the secrets hidden deep in
your soul   Such confessions
have revealed the nation's enemies
Such confessions
have also created lyric poets

他在走　他的周围也有人在走
他们各走各的　走得漫不经心
从一双旧鞋走向一双新鞋
他也在他们中间
但他准确地走向一个旧足球
我说不出来他走的样子
当然也是两只脚　但与与众不同
只有他　坚定不移　目标清楚
两只黑袜子　紧紧地套着小腿
他与别人大不相同
他是走向一只足球去
他必须有特殊的走法
他蹦跳起来

He's walking   others are walking too
each to some place   oblivious
Old shoes new shoes
He walks among them
striding toward an old soccer ball
I can't describe the way he walks
On his feet of course   but different from the others
He's the only one   determined   with a destination
two black socks   tight around his calves
What makes him stand out
is the way he walks
towards a soccer ball
now leaps

深不可测的思想
制造着世界的尺子
但世界只记录
刻在事物表面的尺寸
只记录
额头周围的皱纹

Inscrutable thoughts
create the ruler of the world
but people notice
only the numbers on the surface of things
the wrinkles on the forehead

削苹果的女人
在黄昏中削下一片递给我
我接过来的时候
碰到她有汁的手

Peeling an apple at dusk
she cuts a slice and hands it to me
I take it
from her hand wet with the juice

姑娘们跑进春天浴室
象一棵棵丰满的桃树
把身上的花朵全部打开
这些句子出现
是由于我穿着衣服
在超级市场的电梯上
看见一些粉红色的物资

In springtime girls run into the bathhouse
like plump peach trees
unfolding their blossoms
I write down these lines
in memory of the pink products
I saw from an escalator in the supermarket
fully dressed

主席台上
花朵也穿着毛呢制服
惟一温柔的是倒茶的小姐
当她袅袅走进文件和话筒
为他们沏茶
我们才想起来　这些木偶
也有嘴

On the stage
even the flowers are wearing Mao's wooly uniform
The only tenderness is the tea girl
When she walks among the documents and microphones
pouring tea
we realize   that the puppets
have mouths too

黄金时代就要到了
豹子伸出舌头　虎呲牙裂嘴
狮子抬起前爪　在大地上敲了敲
鹰裂开了眼睛　河流在打磨肚皮
诗人啊　你在何处
快从群众中站出来
你是最后一个
留着尾巴的人

The golden age is coming soon
Leopards stick out their tongues   tigers show their teeth
lions lift their front paws   tap the earth
eagles open their eyes   and rivers grind their bellies
Poets   where are you
Step out of the crowd
You're the last humans
still with a tail

下午的蛋壳碎了
阳光像一群群刚刚孵出来的小鸡
温暖地散落在城市的各处
内心充满光明　我与人生和解
照亮着家庭的暗处
有一只小鸡　跳过百叶窗
落到我的书桌上啄起来
雪白的纸张微微地翘着
像蛋壳的表面
似乎有什么生龙活虎的
就要破壳而出

The eggshell breaks in the afternoon
Light comes in like newly hatched chicks
scattering into the city streets
My heart   full of light   reconciles with life
lights every corner in my house
A little chick   jumps in through my window
pecks at books on my desk
The white paper rises slightly
like an eggshell
as if a tiger or a dragon
is about to break through

干净卫生的广场
不准随地小便的广场
没有妓女和杂种的广场
没有乌鸦和麻雀的广场
旗帜飘扬的广场
同志们的广场
集中着千千万万个喉咙的广场
听不到方言和乡音
四川人不讲四川话
广东人不讲广东话
所有的舌头
都模仿着电台的播音员
用普通话
朗诵汉语

A clean sanitized square
a square where urinating is prohibited
a square with no prostitutes or bastards
a square no crow or sparrow flies across
only red flags fluttering
a square of comrades
where tens of thousands of voices gather
no dialects or sounds from back home
The Sichuanese do not speak Sichuanese
The Cantonese do not speak Cantonese
Every tongue
imitates the radio voice
reciting Chinese
in standard Mandarin

偏远山区的下午
有人读罢课本　在稻草堆旁
想象着一杯热咖啡
想象别处　想象远方
想象着柏油马路和飞机
一头牛在他旁边睡觉
母亲和姑娘们在剥豆
一条狗去了村子的北边
同一时刻在大都市的咖啡馆
另一个人看着玻璃窗外面
灰色的水泥大楼
想念乡村　想念田野上
的野菊花　想念狗　想念
天气　想念着　灰色的马匹
就要　载着秋天的光
飞行　此人和那个
稻草堆旁边的初中生
相距六百二十八公里
这不妨碍他们有同样的
表情　"忧郁，
轻轻地叹了一口气"

Afternoon in a remote mountain village
Someone has just finished reading   against the haystack
fantasizing a cup of hot coffee
somewhere else   far away
fantasizing asphalt streets and airplanes
Next to him a buffalo is sleeping
A mother and some girls are shelling peas
A dog visits the north side of the village
and at the same time in a city café
someone is looking out the window
of a gray concrete building
missing the village   missing the chrysanthemums
in the fields   missing the dogs   missing
the weather   missing the gray horse
about to fly   carrying the autumn
light   this person and the teenager
on the hay are separated by 375 miles
but they share the same melancholy
the same sigh

伤害　不是来自时代
它的巨手从来捉不住我
不是来自那些令我成为诗人的
铁墙　不是那些纸做的绞刑架
不是来自贴在老宅大门上的标语
侮辱我父亲　也侮辱我的青春
不是来自家属被送往流放地的早晨
灰色的秋天　乌云为少年流泪
不是来自我在小瓦房里
拆开第一个少女的
绝交信的时刻
不是来自死亡那边的打击
世界空虚了　在故乡
我第一次看见那神秘的仓库
开门　接纳了外祖母的黑棺材
伤害　不是来自穷母亲
吝啬无比的钱包
我连买一颗玻璃弹的钱
都要不到　不是来自警察
在公园的鱼塘边抓住我
押到大门口示众的时刻
我甚至喜欢在　过去
藏着鬼故事的楼梯里
和那些忠实的霉老鼠
默默地呆着
啊　巨大的伤害
来自那几个拆房子的工人
刚刚从另一个工地抵达

The injury   didn't come from the times
Its giant hand couldn't catch me
It didn't come from the iron wall that made me
a poet   not from the paper gallows
or the slogans on the door of my old house
humiliating my father   and my youth
not from the morning when my family was sent into exile
gray autumn   the clouds crying for the young boy
It didn't come from my hut
where I opened the first rejection letter
from the girl I loved
not from the blow of death
of the empty world   in my old home
I saw the mysterious warehouse for the first time
that opened the door   to let in Grandma's black coffin
The injury   didn't come from my poverty-stricken mother
her tight purse
that wouldn't release a penny
to buy me a marble   not from the cops
who arrested me at the fish pond in the park
and paraded me at the park gate
I still enjoyed the past   where
ghost stories and moldy mice hid
under the staircase
Ah   the huge injury
came from the workers demolishing houses
workers who arrived from another site
to earn their daily twenty yuan
and they were laughing heartily
saying they were going to get drunk after work

每人每天发给二十元人民币
他们大笑着　说下班后要去喝酒
这些酒鬼在一小时之内
就拆掉了
一切

An hour later   these drinkers
had demolished
everything

故乡的井已经干掉
姑娘们依旧似玉如花
当年她们待字闺中
做针线活　低着头
听着一切
今天我在乡村大道上遇见
她们　坐在货车厢里
穿着新买的解放鞋
怀抱着出门的包袱
眼睛发亮
就像一群勘探队员

The well at the old house has dried up
but the girls are still as beautiful as flowers and jade
They used to sit at home
doing needlework   their heads bent
listening
but today
they sit in the cargo train
wearing new military sneakers
clutching a travel pack to their bosoms
their eyes bright
like members of the Geology Scouts

诗人陈平的职业是警察
令人害怕的职业
干些叫人不舒服的事情
他可以随便叫一个正在散步的人
站住！身份证！　陈平
每天穿着警服出现在公园和居民区
站在外面　以一种国家授予的表情
审视人民　小心别出什么差错
大家一边各忙各的　一边
猜测　他又盯上了什么
陈平30岁了　热爱写诗
已经娶妻得子　他常说
俺老家有一座山　一块平原
7棵老槐树　一所小学
水库一个　庙一座　疯子一人
还有一个卫生所　没有监狱
他一只手护住别在腰间的电棒
腾出另一只来写诗
他的诗歌一直是诗歌
抒情诗　印在诗集上哩！
谁也想到是警察叔叔写的！
他抽的烟一直是精装的"红河"牌
许多男人都爱抽这个牌子
他发烟的动作很温存
信任诗人　信任每个男人递来的烟卷
这种古代传下来的信任
使大家常常忘记他要执行的任务
偶尔想到他的手铐
并不忌讳　还有一点好感

Poet Chen Ping is a policeman
a frightening job
that requires him to do uncomfortable things
He can stop any pedestrian
Stop! Your ID!   Chen Ping
appears every day in parks and neighborhoods in his uniform
standing around   watching people
with an expression granted by the nation   an eye out for accidents
Everyone is busy working   while
wondering   what he's up to
Chen Ping is 30   loves poetry
has a wife and a son   He often says
My old home has a mountain   a grassland
seven old elms   an elementary school
a reservoir   a temple   a loony bin
and a clinic   no prison
With one hand he covers the taser at his waist
His other hand writes poetry
His poems are real poems
lyrical ones   that are printed in a book
Who would guess it is written by an Uncle Policeman!
He smokes Red River cigarettes
Many men love this brand
He hands them out gently
trusting other poets   trusting every cigarette handed to him
a trust so ancient
we often forget his job
Sometimes we remember his handcuffs
with no distaste   and even some good feeling

红色的大地在苍天下翻滚
一群农民在地面上忙碌
黄牛在前　男人和妇女紧跟于后
不知道他们在干什么
此地以土豆著名

The red land rolls on beneath the sky
Peasants behind yellow oxen
are tilling the soil   men and women following
No one knows what *they* are doing
This area is known for its potato

司机指着山下一个村庄
脸上有逃亡者的庆幸之色
我曾经在那里喂马 放牛
种土豆 插秧
有一年的春天 四月五日
我与生产队长的女儿
在月光下躺着直到黎明
她是个长辫子
这个叛徒说到这里
看着车头的奔驰车标
忽然沉默了
落日下西岭
攸然群峰瞑

The driver pointed to a village down in the valley
his face shining with the glee of someone who has escaped
I used to herd horses and cattle
used to plant potatoes   grow rice
One year in the spring   April 5th
I slept with my boss' daughter
under the moon till daybreak
She had a long braid
This traitor looked at the Mercedes Benz hood ornament
and fell silent
The sun was setting
and the mountains fell into their shadows

有一天我路过建筑工地
听见一个彝族人在唱歌
那是雨后天晴的六月
火把果红遍云南山岗
我看见这个打工的小伙子
蹲在一包水泥之上
旁边搁着他的大碗
流出了眼泪

That day I passed by the construction site
a Yi worker was singing
It was a sunny June day after a rain shower
Yunnan's mountains were red with torch fruit
I saw a young migrant worker
squat down on a bag of cement
his big rice bowl next to him
tears running down his face

Yi: ethnic minority from Yunnan and Sichuan
torch fruit: a small bumpy fruit shaped like a burning torch

公园的早晨
上千位退休妇女在锻炼
生育完毕　子女们也长大了
放牧在人生的荒原上
碗筷洗得干干净净
得闲　要干些自己的事
冬天的阳光中
一千个母亲翩翩起舞
其中有一位生下了我
我喊了一声妈妈
她们一起回过头来

Morning in the park
Thousands of retired women are exercising
They've given birth   their children are grown
scattered across the wilderness of life
The dishes have been washed
With leisure time they want to do something for themselves
In the winter sunlight
a thousand mothers are dancing
One of them gave birth to me
Mother   I call out
They all turn their heads